this

book belongs to :

There was a little tiger, he was playing with his friends, the fox came over dragging a big round wooden barrel.

The fox said: "My wooden barrel is the most amazing. It can turn one thing into two."
The fox's barrel was very strange, with a wooden handle on one side and a small bell on the other.

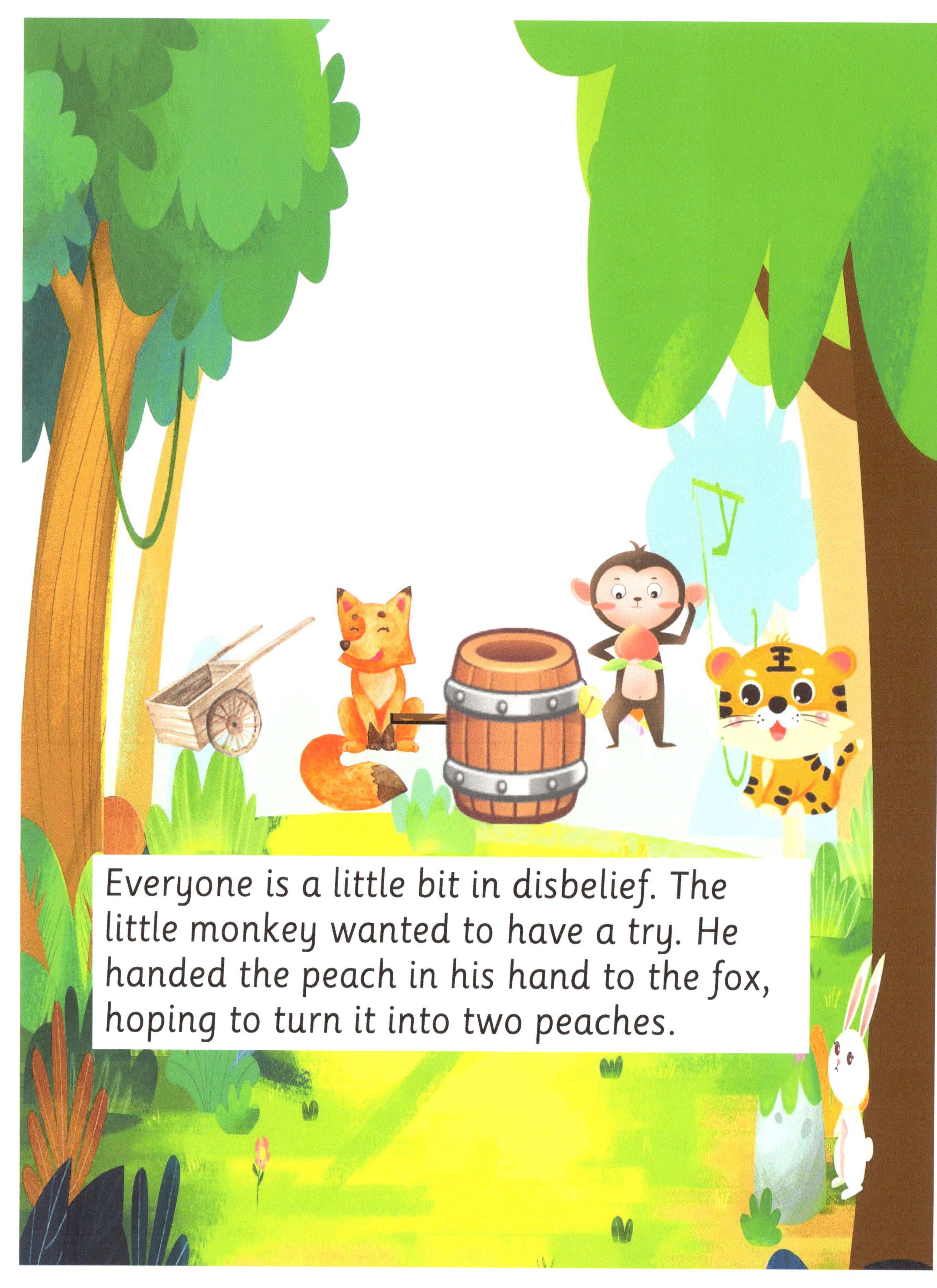

Everyone is a little bit in disbelief. The little monkey wanted to have a try. He handed the peach in his hand to the fox, hoping to turn it into two peaches.

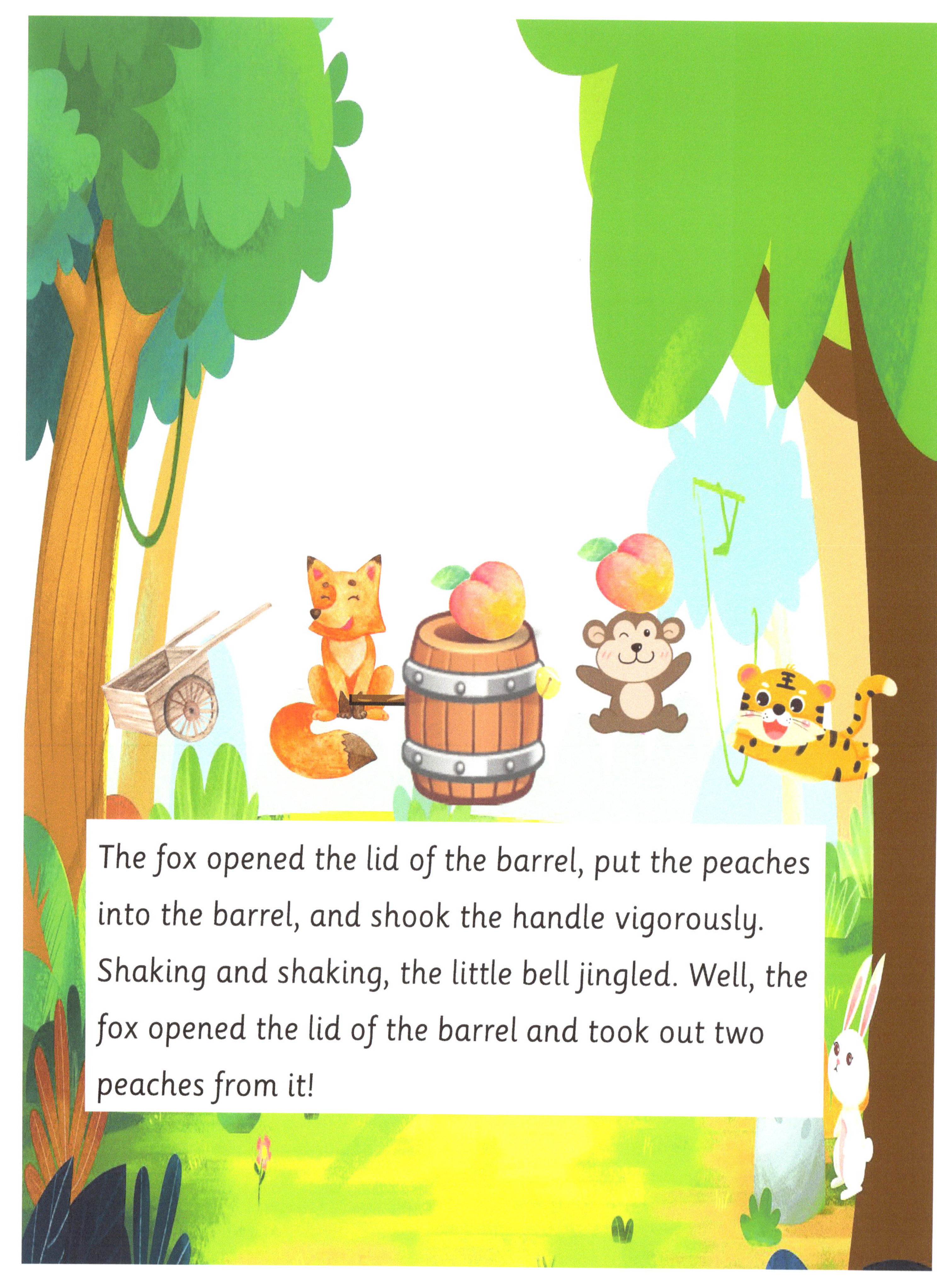

The fox opened the lid of the barrel, put the peaches into the barrel, and shook the handle vigorously. Shaking and shaking, the little bell jingled. Well, the fox opened the lid of the barrel and took out two peaches from it!

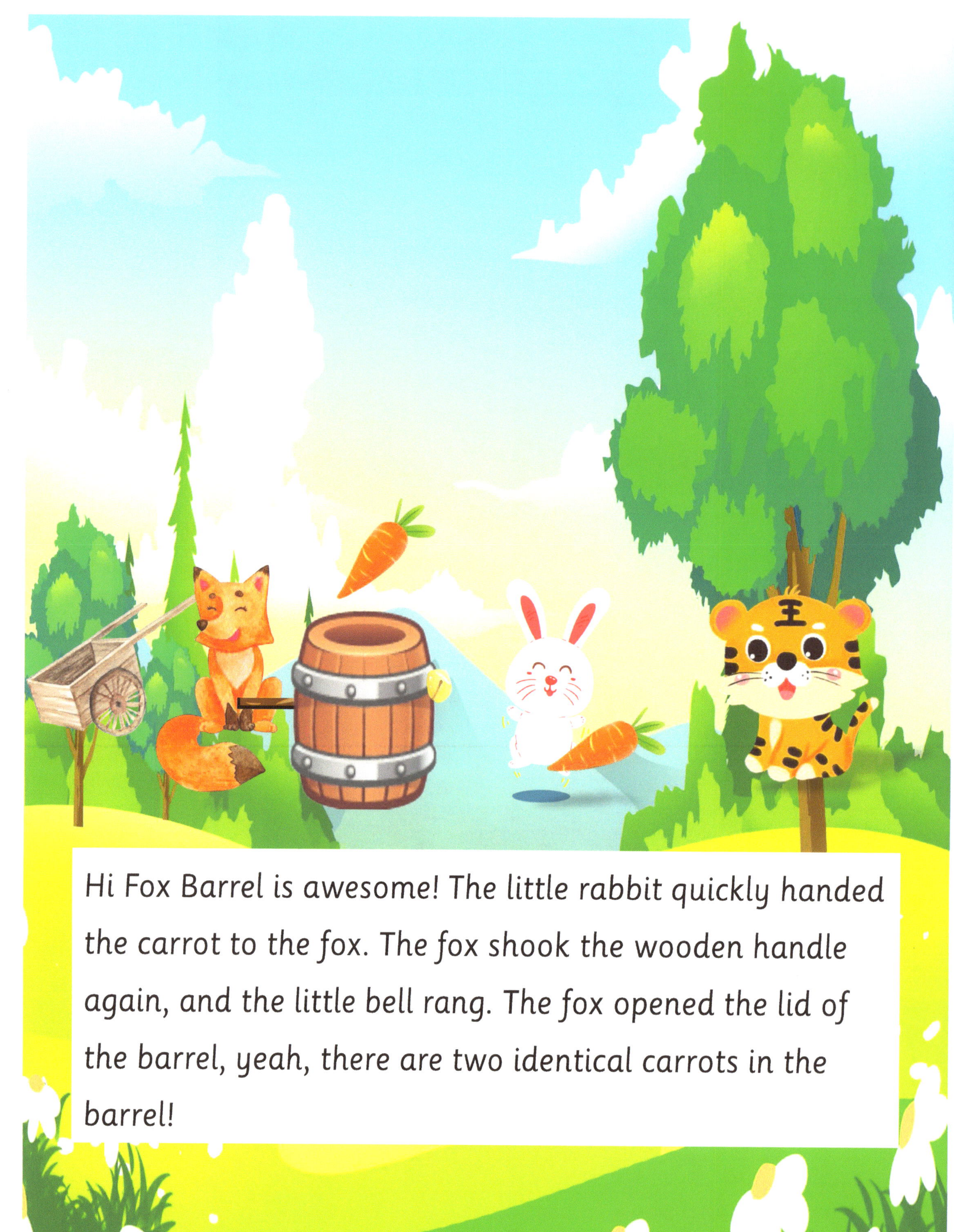

Hi Fox Barrel is awesome! The little rabbit quickly handed the carrot to the fox. The fox shook the wooden handle again, and the little bell rang. The fox opened the lid of the barrel, yeah, there are two identical carrots in the barrel!

The little tiger was in a hurry, he had nothing in his hand, what could he use to make the fox into two?
The little tiger said, "Turn me into two.
When I was sleeping in the woods, I let another little tiger look for meat buns, how wonderful! "

"Okay!" The fox let the cubs jump into the barrel, and shook it. Hey, two little tigers jumped out of the barrel.
王
王

You go find meat buns!
You go find meat buns!
The two little tigers both wanted to sleep and didn't want to look for meat buns.

As they talked, the two little tigers started arguing; when they were arguing, they started fighting. Fight and fight, the two little tigers fight more and more vigorously! Oh yo, when will we finish fighting like this!

The fox looked really anxious, he hurried home and dragged a big square wooden box.

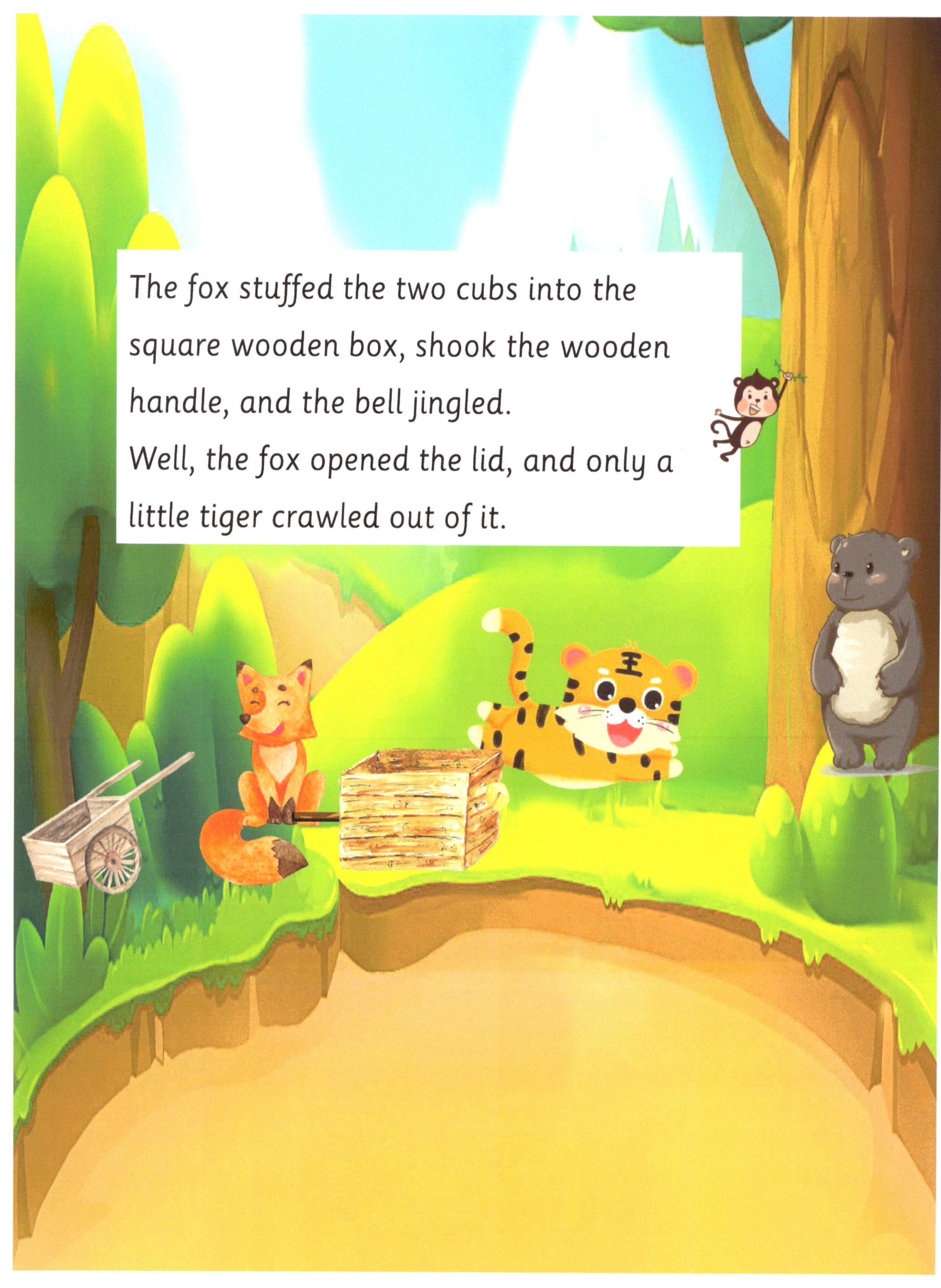

The fox stuffed the two cubs into the square wooden box, shook the wooden handle, and the bell jingled.

Well, the fox opened the lid, and only a little tiger crawled out of it.

The little tiger crawled and said,
"Oh, I'm the only one. I can't go
to the meat buns when I'm
sleeping, and I can't sleep when
I'm looking for the meat buns."
However, the little tiger is still very
happy, because no one will
compete with him for meat buns.

www.ingramcontent.com/pod-product-compliance
Lightning Source LLC
LaVergne TN
LVHW071134160826
845679LV00005B/1280

9798365062542